Numerology

Thorsons First Directions

Numerology

Sonia Ducie

Thorsons
An Imprint of HarperCollinsPublishers
77–85 Fulham Palace Road,
Hammersmith, London W6 8JB

The Thorsons website address is:
www.thorsons.com

Published by Thorsons 2000
Text derived from *Principles of Numerology* published by Thorsons 1998

10 9 8 7 6 5 4 3 2 1

Text copyright © Sonia Ducie 2000
Copyright © Thorsons 2000

Sonia Ducie asserts the moral right to be identified as the author of this work

Editor: Jo Kyle
Design: Wheelhouse Creative
Photography by PhotoDisc Europe Ltd.

A catalogue record for this book is available from the British Library

ISBN 0 0071 0333 6

Printed and bound in Hong Kong

Contents

Numerology

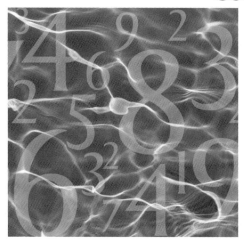

is the psychology, philosophy

and science of numbers

What is Numerology?

Numerology is the psychology, philosophy and science of numbers. It can be described as a study of the mind – where each number offers you insights into your psychological patterns. It is also a philosophy – it offers you deep insights into the realms of existence. Numerology can also be described as a science: one that can help you to solve certain problems or situations in your life or to explore your potential. Numbers influence your life in every way and Numerology can help you to understand more about life in general.

   To practice Numerology you need to be able to add up simple numbers but you don't need to be a mathematician.

Working out the numbers is only one part of Numerology, whilst using intuitive interpretation is another. Numerology is a method by which you can develop your intuition, as you learn to trust your response to the impression you get when you 'read' the numbers. When you have been working with numbers for a while you really get a feel for them and start to see the overall picture – the numbers talk to you!

The principles of Numerology

In Numerology all life is governed by the numbers 1 to 9. Any number above 9 can be added to form a single digit between 1 and 9.
For example, if you are adding up the number 38, then $3 + 8 = 11$, and $1 + 1 = 2$, so the final number is 2.

Numerology is applied to your date of birth and your names. Each letter equates to a number, which when totalled gives additional information about your life. From A – Z these add up from 1 to 26. For example, $A = 1$, $P = 7$, etc.

Each number has many qualities, strengths and weaknesses, and negative and positive influences are associated with each cycle 1 to 9. Negative influences or qualities do not mean that something is bad; they are weaknesses that are as important as your positive influences and strengths, because you can work on them to make them stronger. For example, if you have the influence of 4 in your chart you may be lazy. You may regard this as a negative quality, but by being aware of it you can start to take action (if you choose) to transform this quality into a strength.

You have a combination of positive and negative influences in your chart, and you use them to different degrees from day to day, and during different times of your life. For example, you may be a really positive person, but because of a current trauma you may display a majority of negative qualities or influences in your chart for a time.

Cycles and trends

Everything in life works out at its own pace and rhythm; you have your own personal rhythm or cycles too, as indicated by the numbers in your chart. Numerologists believe we live out our lives in nine-year cycles. Getting to know your own numerological cycles can help you to fulfil the potential of all events and in all areas of your life.

The first six years of any of your nine-year cycles are related to physical experiences – you are out participating in life. Your seventh year is a year for bringing together the wisdom of the experiences in your previous six years. During your eighth year you re-evaluate your previous seven years, and indeed every nine-year cycle before that. Finally, in your ninth year, you are in a year of completing and beginning new ideas and situations. Often when you get to your eighth and ninth years of your cycle you may find there can be great changes in your life – these changes may be emotional, mental or spiritual as well as physical.

From your age number (*see page* 21) you can see what experiences may occur during your nine-year cycle.

Uses of Numerology

Numbers influence every area of our lives. You can use them on a personal level to gain greater clarity about yourself, and your purpose in life. You can, for example, apply Numerology to find out more about your health, your career and your relationships, and to highlight your talents and gifts.

Numerology can be used in the business world too. The name of your company and its birth date (that is the first day of trading) can be put into Numerological order to see its natural trends and cycles.

You can use Numerology in recruitment to see whether the job matches the person you are employing. If you are launching new products then Numerology highlights the maximum potential for the timing of the launch, and the best possible product name.

Numbers can also be added up to represent the important influences of the year you live in. For example, 2000 adds up to 2, and this 2 – the number for sharing, co-operation, balance and choice, will influence all the experiences that the world has in this year.

Numerology can also be applied to advertising, features in newspapers, politics, religion, economics, the weather, indeed anything in life, to help you understand what is truly being communicated.

The History of Numerology

Throughout history, numbers have enabled mankind to produce an understanding of life, how it was in the past, how it is now, and how it will be … via the ability to interpret the cycles and trends and the qualities contained within each number.

Pythagoras and Plato

Pythagoras was one of the early Numerologists and masters. He was a Greek mathematician and philosopher who taught his students to develop their intuition at his School of Mysteries in southern Italy around 600BC. Pythagoras believed that numbers were the 'essence of all life'.

Plato was a philosopher and was responsible for recording much of the information about Numerology that he learned from Pythagoras. This simple and powerful system was later passed down through common usage.

Other systems

There are many different systems or traditions in Numerology. These systems vary but man has always used his predicament and collective circumstances to interpret the numbers according to the world in which he has lived, and lives, and according to his needs. For example, up to the middle of the 20th century many Numerologists used the system 1 to 7, and 7 was the number for completion. People died much younger in the old days, and many did not live to the age of 70(7). Seven was then the number for a priest, spiritual healer, or a mystic with special powers to perform ritual magic or heal the sick.

Today, Humanity's needs have changed and are constantly changing, which is reflected in the numbers we use. There is more time to focus on desires and dreams and emotional well-being, rather than physical survival. This is reflected in Numerology, which today recognizes the system based on 1 to 9, and 1 to 81(9), etc.

Numerology also recognizes Master or 'Mirror Numbers' today, which are 11, 22, 33, 44, 55, 66, 77, 88 and 99. These intensify the lessons or influences from the individual number, and indicate extreme qualities or gifts that can be used to help others.

Methods of interpretation

Many cultures have used Numerology and their methods have been passed down and given modern interpretations and meanings by people of today. For example, over the centuries Hindus have incorporated Numerology into their beliefs and superstitions, and used it for prediction. Often they used the method called divination – or the calculation of numbers to predict an exact time or outcome of events.

The ancient Tibetans also used methods of divination, which were employed by their Oracles (or mystics) who predicted the future, particularly for the State.

China still has its book of insight or prediction and this is called the I *Ching*, or the 'Book of Changes'. It was written about 5,000 years ago and is an ancient book of wisdom.

Numerology was also used in ancient Egypt. Numerologists have gained detailed information about life at that time by translating hieroglyphic symbols. Numerology was also used statistically when the great mathematicians designed the pyramids, using numerological measurements in symmetry with the rays of the sun.

The ancient Greeks used a method of Numerology called Sacred Geometry. In Sacred Geometry shapes such as circles, squares, triangles, etc, are used to determine the number they represent within an area governed by a symbol. This method was used to count grain; by simply glancing at its shape, or geometry, it was easy to determine how much grain was available.

The Kabbalah is the Hebrew book based on esoteric understanding of the Bible, which uses the alphabet (based on the phonetic sounds) to find information about past, present and future for an individual from the names given at birth. These letters are transcribed into numbers and from that insights are given. They designate odd numbers as masculine and active, and even numbers as female and passive.

Working out your Chart

Your key numbers

The two most important numbers influencing your life are your Personality Number and your Life Path Number, both taken from your date of birth. Both these numbers portray strengths and weaknesses, positive and negative attributes, and highlight your maximum potential in life.

Your Personality Number reveals gifts and qualities that are often very different from those associated with your Life Path Number (unless these two numbers are the same). Sometimes the qualities from your Personality Number are stronger influences over your life than your Life Path Number. At other times in your life your Life Path Number has a more powerful influence over your experiences.

The next most important influence in your life is from your Wisdom Number, taken from your full name, which gives you practical gifts to use in your life. Finally, your age is also an influence over the kind of experiences you will have during that year.

Your Personality Number

Your personality portrays some characteristics that you inherited from your parents and were born with and some that you develop as life goes on. Your Personality Number is taken from the exact date in the month you were born. For instance, if you were born on the 9th, then you have the influence of the 9 in your personality. If you were born on a double digit date add the two numbers together:

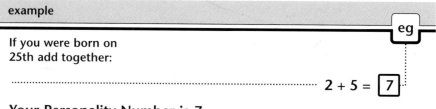

example

If you were born on
25th add together:

.... 2 + 5 = $\boxed{7}$ eg

Your Personality Number is 7

Life Path Number

Your Life Path Number highlights your direction, or greater purpose in life; bringing awareness to this aspect can help you achieve clarity about your life, and give you a deeper insight into your full potential. You find this number by adding up the whole date of your birth.

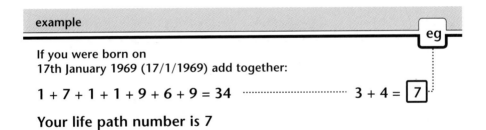

example

eg

If you were born on 17th January 1969 (17/1/1969) add together:

1 + 7 + 1 + 1 + 9 + 6 + 9 = 34 ·················· **3 + 4 =** 7

Your life path number is 7

Your Wisdom Number

The Wisdom Number highlights practical qualities or gifts you have or may accumulate, and can use in your lifetime. It is the wisdom of knowledge gained by experience that leads you to develop practical gifts, which you can use to help yourself, or others. To work out this number you simply translate each letter into numbers (*see page* 20) and add together the whole name on your birth certificate. This includes any names registered including middle names. (If you do not have a birth certificate then go by the names first known to you.)

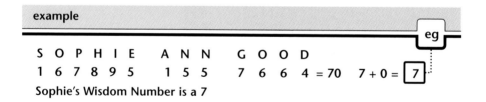

example

S	O	P	H	I	E		A	N	N		G	O	O	D			eg
1	6	7	8	9	5		1	5	5		7	6	6	4	= 70	7 + 0 =	7

Sophie's Wisdom Number is a 7

Your married name (add up your first, middle names and surname) brings extra qualities, which you learn about from your partner, but does not replace the influence of the names on your birth certificate.

Qualities within your name

You can take each of your individual names – Christian or first, middle, and surname or family name – and work out the number for each of them. The most important names are the ones on your birth certificate.

When you look at all the numbers in your names, notice if there are any that are repeated – you may have lots of 4s or 7s, for instance. This means that these are qualities you are strongly working with and which will influence you greatly. Also notice what numbers are missing from your chart. These can indicate qualities you need to focus on to make you stronger, or they can be strong already, because you have been working with those qualities for a long time.

If your name has a prefix, eg MacClean, then include all the letters as part of the surname or family name. Similarly, double-barreled names or names like Van Der Holland are generally considered to be all part of your surname. Names like Anne-Marie are also considered to be one name.

Alphabet chart

Here is a translation of the alphabet into numbers which you may like to study and memorize so that you can work out names and words quickly and easily. Numerology is easier to apply when you don't need to think too hard about how to 'work it out', because when you are relaxed it flows, and you enjoy it more.

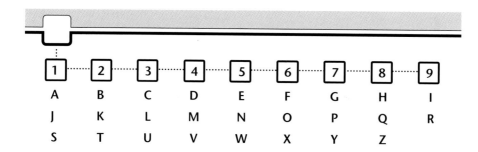

1	2	3	4	5	6	7	8	9
A	B	C	D	E	F	G	H	I
J	K	L	M	N	O	P	Q	R
S	T	U	V	W	X	Y	Z	

Your age

Your age exerts an influence over each year it governs. It is worked out by simply adding your age up to form a single number between 1 to 9.

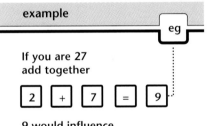

The Meanings
of Numbers

The following chapter explains many qualities and meanings of the numbers 1 to 9, and indicates ways in which these numbers can influence your life.

Time of birth

If you were born just after midnight then it is possible that you may identify strongly with the qualities from the day before. For example, if you were born on the 15th at 1am, then you may be influenced by 14 or 5 (1+4), so look up this number too.

Countries

At the start of each section there are the names of some countries. These countries may share the same number that is in your chart, or carry a similar vibration of energy. When you visit a country that you identify with it may help you with your personal development and growth, and can expand your knowledge about the world you live in.

number
one

One is the number for new beginnings, new life, new ways of doing things, new opportunities and new goals, and it is also the number for destruction (for breaking down old patterns, or old ways of doing things).

☐ Countries

Israel, Turkey, Egypt, India, Pakistan, Afghanistan, Caribbean.

☐ Famous 1s

The Late Diana, Princess of Wales, Sophia Loren, Jack Nicholson, Tom Wolfe.

Personality

▢ Positive

With a 1 personality you are highly creative, with a driving ambition towards your goals. You exude energy and vitality and have staying power to go for what you want, with a get up and go that makes you strive for more.

You enjoy intellectual stimulation and you enjoy learning; you need mental and physical challenges.

You can be compulsive about life, and continue to do things just for the sake of it. Equally, you are good at finding new things to do to stimulate your body and mind.

You can be a pioneer, who loves to climb mountains or to explore virgin territory, where you can be stimulated by new life and discover new things.

With a 1, you are a strong individual and you often feel the need to find your own sense of individuality. This may show itself in the way you dress, the work you do, or the way you speak. You also enjoy your own company, and love to do things on your own.

▢ Negative

With a 1 personality you are a detached person, and you may fear any kind of intimacy. You can also get 'stuck' emotionally, and be unable or unwilling to relate to people. You can be extremely self-centred, and you are very good at looking after number one.

Your ability to focus can be a problem when you get stuck on one thing and refuse to budge. The harder people try to dig you out of a rut, the more you may insist on digging your heels in.

With a 1 you can be withdrawn, lonely and self-pitying. You can be fearful about not being able to achieve your goals, which in itself can hold you back from trying. Alternatively, you can also be overpowering in your drive for your goals, and you may 'walk all over people' who you think are holding you back.

You may be lacking in your own individuality, and you may like to have others around you who are strong individuals. You can also feel challenged and threatened at times, when others assert their own individuality.

Life Path number **one**

☐ Positive

With a 1 Life Path you are learning to work towards your independence. You are very directional, and know where you are going from one moment to the next in your life. You are a born leader.

☐ Negative

You may want to be led instead of taking the lead. You may be dependent, lost without direction or drive and want others to do things for you. You may be dictatorial and use your leadership in selfish ways that are only to your advantage.

Wisdom

☐ Positive

With a 1 Wisdom Number you are able to bring in your practical gift of courage when breaking down old ways of doing things, and have courage to face new situations. The number 1 is associated with the 'will', and the strength of will to carry things forward on your own, and as an independent person. You have an ability to overcome obstacles and like to include everyone in your life and treat everybody equally.

☐ Negative

You may be arrogant and exclude others, believing yourself to be superior. You may enjoy being destructive and use this for your own ends. You may withdraw as your line of defence.

How the number **one** influences your:

☐ Health

You enjoy physical exercise to help keep you fit and mentally alert, although you can become over focused and preoccupied with this too. At times you may resist exercise as you remain focused solely on other things.

☐ Relationships

You are striving towards independence, therefore you may attract partners who are also independent, or a dependent partner who can teach you about involvement. You may go for a long time without getting deeply involved within a relationship.

☐ Career

You are a born leader and so may be a leader in politics, fashion, art, music, in fact a leader in any field. You may be an inventor, or a brilliant designer, or a creative ideas person.

☐ Finance

Money is not your main concern – you work because you love what you do, and you would even work for very little. You may not necessarily be 'good' at handling money because it isn't the most important thing in your life.

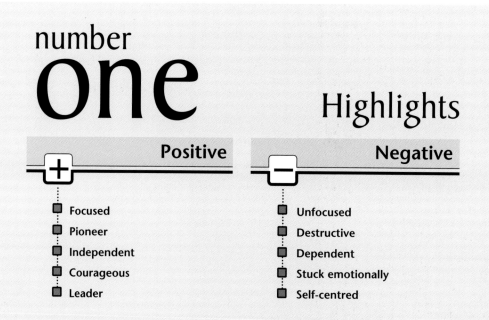

number
one
Highlights

+ Positive	− Negative
Focused	Unfocused
Pioneer	Destructive
Independent	Dependent
Courageous	Stuck emotionally
Leader	Self-centred

number
two

Two is the number for balance and decision making.

☐ Countries

France, Germany, Africa, Tibet, United Kingdom, Venezuela.

☐ Famous 2s

HRH The Prince of Wales, Marvyn Gaye, Madonna, Phil Collins.

Personality

number
two

☐ Positive

With a 2 personality you are highly sensitive and intuitive and have a gentle, quiet nature. You make a good listener.

You are able to nurture and take care of others – like a mother – and you love to love others. You can be passive, soft and even pliable, and you do not get het up about unimportant issues. You are good at making decisions.

You are placid, stable and able to steady others when they have problems. You are able to see both points of view or both sides of an argument. You do not like to hurt people.

With a 2 personality you are tolerant, and like sharing yourself with others. This can be sharing emotional exchange, sharing your possessions, sharing ideas, sharing your home and so on.

You often like to compare yourself to others. This happens naturally because you like to see how you can relate to them, and how you can get along together.

You enjoy quiet pursuits and you may have musical gifts, which you use for yourself or to bring happiness to others.

❑ Negative

With a 2 personality, you can be a cautious person who takes life very slowly (although at times you can 'throw caution to the wind'). You may be fearful of making decisions.

You can be defensive and confrontational. You can also be highly disagreeable and awkward when you want to be, and you can be touchy at times.

You can be uncaring towards others and when they need you (especially emotionally) you may walk away.

You can be extremely moody, and you are very good at sulking. With a 2 you can be covert with your actions and you may even be deceitful. You can also lack diplomacy and be tactless at times.

You can be highly unco-operative, and you like to get your own way. You may also be unable and unwilling to share your life with others, as you are still learning about 'give and take'.

With a 2 you are always comparing yourself with others, to see how you can make yourself feel good, or better than them.

Life Path

number two

☐ Positive

With a 2 Life Path, you are learning to find balance within all areas of your life. You are working towards finding inner peace and calm, and learning to balance your emotions so that you have emotional stability.

☐ Negative

There may be no sense of balance in your life. You may be emotionally weak, shaky or unbalanced, and your emotions may 'fly all over the place'. There may be general disharmony within your relationships as there is within yourself.

Wisdom

☐ **Positive**
Your practical gift is the ability to share your love and wisdom with others; whether that be with those close to you, your community, or the world at large.

☐ **Negative**
You may be insensitive, uncaring and unable to share knowledge you have gained from your experiences with others.

How the number two influences your:

☐ **Health**

You are very aware about keeping a balance in your life, and try to do this by taking physical exercise, eating healthily and getting plenty of sleep, etc. You may be very interested in complementary medicine and healing.

☐ **Relationships**

You are someone who is in love with being 'in love'. You are warm, loving and giving, and expect others to be the same. You may be emotionally demanding and over emotional at times.

☐ **Career**

You would make a good judge or diplomat. You are an ideal 'middleman', agent, or a mediator within any organization or team. You would also feel at home as a counsellor, and doing any community work or in the caring profession.

◻ Finance

You can at times be overcautious with your money and hoard it. At other times you can be extravagant, particularly when pandering to your emotional needs. Having balanced emotions can help to keep your bank account balanced too.

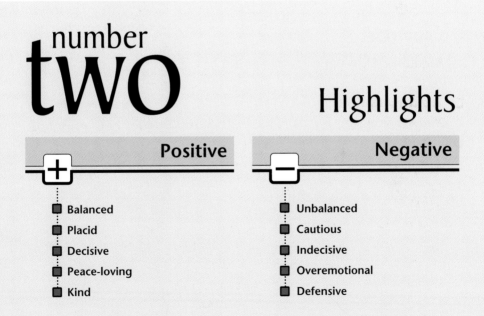

number
two

Highlights

Positive

- Balanced
- Placid
- Decisive
- Peace-loving
- Kind

Negative

- Unbalanced
- Cautious
- Indecisive
- Overemotional
- Defensive

t^{number}hree

Number 3 is for expansion, moving forward, for protection and abundance.

❏ Countries

Australia, Denmark, Luxembourg, Iceland, Vietnam, England, USA.

❏ Famous 3s

Katherine Hepburn, John Travolta, Barbara Walters.

Personality number three

▢ Positive

With a 3 personality you are highly active both mentally and physically, and are usually bright and intelligent. You are demonstrative, and fun is a part of your everyday routine. You have a witty, well-developed sense of humour that makes you very attractive.

People like you because you have a sunny, easy-going nature that uplifts them. You are confident and outgoing, with an endless supply of free-flowing energy which you lavish on yourself and others. You just love social contact.

You may feel the most 'alive' in the 'great outdoors' and may enjoy camping, or activities such as riding or trekking, etc.

You may have a strong connection and interest in mysticism (covering any aspect of healing). You may also have strong religious beliefs.

When challenges arise in your life, you can usually cope really well because you simply take life in your stride.

☐ Negative

With the 3 personality you may experience a great deal of mental confusion at times.

You may be an untidy person who often 'gets in a mess', or leaves a mess behind you. For example, at home you can be messy, but you may also find yourself in 'messy' situations with relationships.

You may lead a chaotic life, rushing around and doing everything at once. You may lack the ability to focus on the important issues in your life, and end up doing things in a superficial way. With a 3 you may also have a tendency to overwork, or overdo things at times.

Sometimes, however, you can be so 'laid back', relaxed and carefree that you don't get around to doing very much. You may be scattered and lack boundaries or structure in your life.

You may suffer from a lack of confidence, which may stop you from doing things at times. You can be highly critical of yourself and others.

With a 3, you may lose your sense of humour, or your enthusiasm about your life.

Life Path

number three

☐ **Positive**

With the 3 Life Path, you are learning about self-expression and creativity. Self-expression can be through your emotions, through physical activity, through your work, and through communicating. Your creativity greatly needs to be expressed, and one way you may do this is by using your hands. You are also a flexible person, who can adapt easily to changes in your life.

☐ **Negative**

When you are strongly working through the negative elements of this number you may be unable to express yourself in one or many areas of your life. Your creativity may also be blocked. When your expression and creativity are blocked it can affect every area of your life. You may not adapt easily to changing circumstances around you.

Wisdom

number
three

☐ Positive

With a 3 influencing your Wisdom Number, your practical gift is a positive mind. Keeping your mind positive means you help to create positive events in your life, and help keep others positive too.

☐ Negative

You may be burdened with negative thoughts, which may prevent your life from flowing in the best possible way.

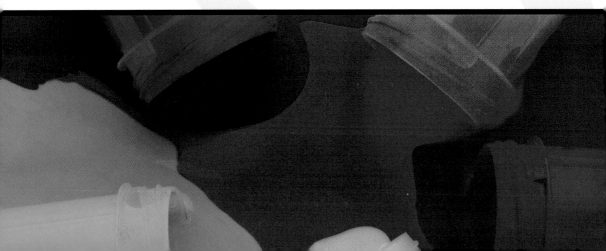

How the number **three** influences your:

☐ **Health**

Generally, you are relaxed and laid back. A relaxed attitude helps you avoid taking on too much stress in your life, because you let go of worrying. This in turn helps you to stay healthy in the long run.

☐ **Relationships**

You are a 'good time babe' and you may generally enjoy superficial or brief encounters. However, when you feel it's time to commit yourself to a partner you will happily do so.

☐ **Career**

A career that enables you to express your creativity appeals to you; you may be an artist, a chef, a gardener, a massage therapist or a writer. You may be involved with religion or mysticism, or you may well be a comedian, entertainer, dancer or lecturer.

☐ Finance

Number 3 has a strong association with abundance. When you have the potential for so much self-expression, and when all your energy and enthusiasm are channelled into positive creativity, money can simply flow.

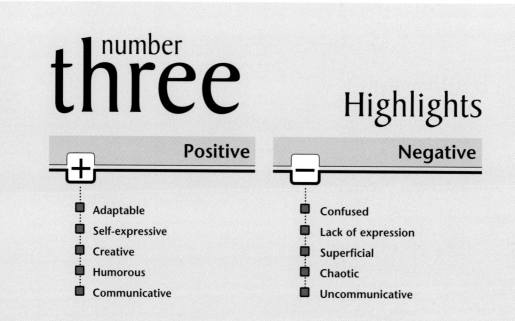

number
three

Highlights

+ Positive	− Negative
Adaptable	Confused
Self-expressive	Lack of expression
Creative	Superficial
Humorous	Chaotic
Communicative	Uncommunicative

f number four

Four is the number for foundations, grounding, systems – law and order.

☐ Countries

Italy, Myanmar, Columbia.

☐ Famous 4s

The Dalai Lama, Richard Gere, Oprah Winfrey, Martina Navratilova.

Personality

number four

☐ **Positive**

With a 4 personality you are someone who likes routine. For you, knowing your routine is going to be the same offers you great security, and can help you to feel safe.

You are a home lover and a home maker. You like stability and you tend to think in terms of your long-term needs and future security. You enjoy material comforts, and like to materialize things, bringing your ideas into form.

You are happy to work hard to provide the lifestyle you require. You are a highly capable and determined person, and people know they can rely on you to follow through once you have made a commitment or promise. You make a loyal friend, and although it may take you time to make friends, once you have established a rapport or a bond, then it's usually for life.

You are tactile and earthy. You enjoy being in the woods and mountains, and you like to feel connected to the land. You can be passionate and creative, and you are generally committed to your life and making it work.

☐ Negative

With a 4 personality you may dislike monotony. It is one thing having a routine, but it's another when life seems to drag on the same every day.

Change can be difficult for you to handle, because whilst you may welcome a change it can make you feel insecure and uncomfortable.

You may be a workaholic who hardly stops to eat. You may also be fearful about your long-term security at times. To compensate, you may develop an all-consuming preoccupation with material possessions, which you think can help you feel safe.

Alternatively, you may not wish to put your 'roots down' or to consolidate your life, and you may go through life with no real material security.

You may be lazy and unproductive at times, and you may lack the persistence to carry things through. You can also be very impractical.

You may find it difficult to form solid friendships, or be unprepared to put effort into the ones you have already.

Life Path number four

☐ Positive

With your 4 Life Path your main direction or lessons in life are to learn to take responsibility for yourself and to learn how to master endurance, so that you can carry on no matter what. You are also learning to find satisfaction in the ordinariness of everyday living.

☐ Negative

With a 4 influencing your Life Path you may display dissatisfaction within your life in general. You may be irresponsible and give up easily when challenges come your way.

Wisdom

number **four**

O **Positive**

With a 4 Wisdom Number, your practical gift is your ability to be able to consolidate your life. You can take what you have made of your life, and build upon those experiences to make your life more solid.

O **Negative**

The negative aspect of your 4 Wisdom Number means you may not be able to 'put your life down on paper' or make it feel secure. Perhaps you do not have a firm base to work from.

How the number four influences your:

☐ **Health**

You handle health problems in a practical way as you are a 'down-to-earth' person. You simply get on with your life each day by doing the best you can to help yourself get better.

☐ **Relationships**

When you have a steady relationship it helps you to feel safe and secure, and you are willing to put in much effort towards maintaining that union. You like getting physical with your partner and enjoy the passion of creativity together.

☐ **Career**

You seek work that can offer you long-term security. You may be a housekeeper, a herbalist, a farmer. You may be a builder, a security officer, or work for an insurance or property company. Alternatively, you may work for a financial institution, or be an accountant.

Finance

You are prepared to work hard for your money. You like buying material possessions but you also like saving money. You may like to invest money in property or 'secure' bonds, which helps you to feel safe.

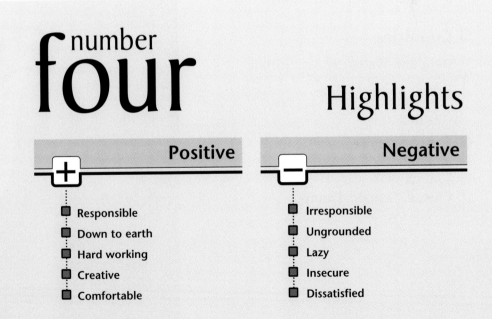

number
four

Highlights

Positive

- Responsible
- Down to earth
- Hard working
- Creative
- Comfortable

Negative

- Irresponsible
- Ungrounded
- Lazy
- Insecure
- Dissatisfied

number five

Number 5 is the number for experimentation, language, concrete knowledge or facts and change.

☐ Countries

Belgium, Wales, Spain, Sudan, Brazil, Saudi Arabia.

☐ Famous 5s

Mick Jagger, Paul Simon, John Cleese, Donald Trump.

Personality

☐ Positive

With a 5 personality you have a fascination with life. You have an inquisitive mind, and you are always asking a lot of questions. You thrive on change and new opportunities, and you love to 'go with the flow'.

You love to learn about different subjects, and you have rounded up a little information about most things in life. To you 'variety is the spice of life'.

You also have energy and a zest for life. Life is an adventure and you go out looking for it; you may love bungee jumping, white water rafting, scuba diving and skiing.

With a 5 you are a highly magnetic or attractive person. You are popular, and people are fascinated by you, and you are also fascinated by them! You ooze charm, and you enjoy flirting with everyone.

You are a spontaneous person, and can be as changeable as the wind. You love travelling; new people, new lands, new situations, new life … so much to see and so much to do … non-stop.

☐ Negative

With a 5 personality you can be extremely restless. When your life gets 'in a rut' you are prone to making fast and sometimes irrational decisions, for example, walking out of your job or a relationship.

Your impulsive nature can make you unreliable and unpredictable at times. You may be prone to stormy moods and verbal outbursts. You may also fear change. You may refuse to get on with life, and procrastinate.

You are also prone to setting yourself restrictions. For example, you may say, 'I can only go out with somebody who has green eyes.' You may be scared to 'open up' to life, and use restrictions as a 'safety net' because it is overwhelming to realize there can be so much choice.

You may sometimes be prone to addictions – chocolate, food, alcohol, drugs, sex, people, etc. You may also be abusive to people and towards things, and you can be very pushy.

With a 5 you may lack energy, vitality and enthusiasm, and lose your fascination for life, at times.

Life Path

number
five

□ **Positive**

With your 5 Life Path, you are learning to express yourself through communication. Communication is important because it is the method by which you connect with others. You are also learning about commitment within all areas of your life. Another lesson is to learn about freedom. This may mean you need your freedom, and you need to learn to allow others their freedom too.

□ **Negative**

With a 5 Life Path you may avoid commitment because you fear involvement or because you feel trapped (and you think you may lose your freedom). You may be unable to enjoy the freedom to communicate with others.

Wisdom

number
five

☐ Positive

With a 5 influencing your Wisdom Number, your practical gift is your clarity of mind. You can use this gift to help others get clarity in their lives too.

☐ Negative

With a 5 Wisdom Number you may experience mental confusion and, like a fog, be unable to see the way ahead clearly.

How the five number influences your:

☐ **Health**

You are an active person and during times of illness you like to find out the facts, and get any 'niggle' about your health checked out. You love most forms of exercise but particularly skiing, swimming, tennis and riding.

☐ **Relationships**

You are fun-loving, adventurous and lively and you may seek out a partner who shares the same zest for life. You may also like a partner who can offer you intellectual stimulation.

☐ **Career**

You excel in anything related to the communications industry; public relations, marketing, sales, journalism, travel, computing, etc. You can also make a brilliant investigator, manager, writer or even a dancer. You may be a teacher or you may work with languages.

☐ Finance

Once you have learned to commit to life and to a career you may earn plenty of money – and fast. However, you may also spend it as fast as you earn it. Nevertheless, you are magnetic and there is usually more where the last lot came from.

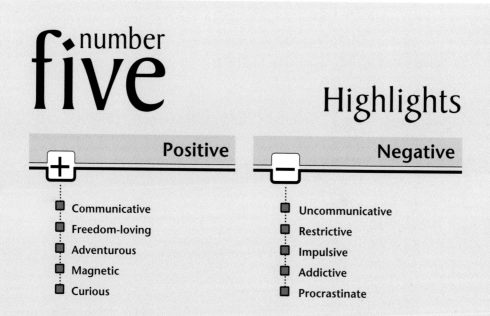

number
five

Highlights

+ Positive	**− Negative**
Communicative	Uncommunicative
Freedom-loving	Restrictive
Adventurous	Impulsive
Magnetic	Addictive
Curious	Procrastinate

◆number
six

Number 6 is the number for harmony, commitment, relationships, marriage and family.

☐ Countries

Mexico, Thailand, Russia, New Zealand, Japan, Norway, Canada, Iran.

☐ Famous 6s

Joan of Arc, George Michael, Howard Hughes.

Personality

number six

☐ Positive

With a 6 personality your home is one of the most important aspects within your life, bringing you great joy and emotional security.

Family life is essential to your enjoyment of life; you enjoy being part of a group. You are a carer, who loves to look after and nurture people, and you make a good listener.

You are a loving, warm, generous person and you are good at giving. You are highly perceptive and can see other people's needs. You are a crusader with a keen sense of justice.

You have a strong desire for the good things in life – good food and wine, fine art, harmonious music, etc. You have an appreciation of beauty and aesthetics, and you are sensitive to your environment.

You can be an idealist and perfectionist at times, but you also like to meander through life and just 'let yourself go'. You like to go deeply into life; in your relationships, at work, etc. You find it relatively easy to commit yourself fully.

☐ Negative

With a 6 personality you may resent your duties, and resent looking after and caring for people.

You can be overgenerous, and help everyone who comes your way. Perhaps you need to learn to say 'no' sometimes and prevent yourself from becoming a willing doormat and being taken for granted. You may also be a moaning martyr who continues to help people, whilst letting the whole world know what a saint you are!

You can be interfering at times, and you may want to get overinvolved with people's lives, particularly emotionally. You may also be overemotional at times, and very 'needy'. When someone hurts you emotionally you may like to 'get your own back' and even be vengeful at times.

You can go very deeply into life and may even develop obsessions about things – your work, your health, the way you look – or you may become obsessive about a person.

You are also prone to jealousy. Sometimes when you are jealous it is because you are not acknowledging your own gifts or seeing goodness within yourself.

Life Path   six number

□ Positive

The main influences from 6 are your ability to take responsibility for the group (your family, community, etc) and to recognize group needs. Also to use your wisdom to help yourself and others, and to use your gift of healing. You are learning about all these qualities to help you with your life.

□ Negative

With a 6 Life Path you may recognize others' needs but only be interested in getting your own needs met. You may find it difficult to take on family responsibilities or refuse to take on group responsibilities. You may feel uncomfortable sharing, or using your wisdom to help heal yourself and others.

Wisdom

☐ **Positive**

With a 6 Wisdom Number, you have a practical gift of tolerance which helps you to learn to 'live' with people and accept life as it is.

☐ **Negative**

You may react to challenges by being intolerant, and not accepting other people and their feelings as they are.

How the **six** number influences your:

☐ Health

You are generally very aware of your diet – food is an important focus for you. Wholefoods or organic foods may feature strongly in your diet. You like the 'good life' and you may be inclined to overindulge yourself in food.

☐ Relationships

You like to get emotionally involved with your partner and to go deeply into the relationship by making a commitment. You are one of nature's true romantics.

☐ Career

You can make a good charity worker, or community carer. You may succeed in the litigation field, and can excel as a counsellor. You may work in the medical profession. You may also be a (graphic) artist, beautician, musician or singer, writer, or a designer of any sort.

☐ Finance

You earn money not simply for the sake of it, but as a way of providing the good things in life. You are good at providing money to care for yourself, but a part of you may also like someone else to provide money for you.

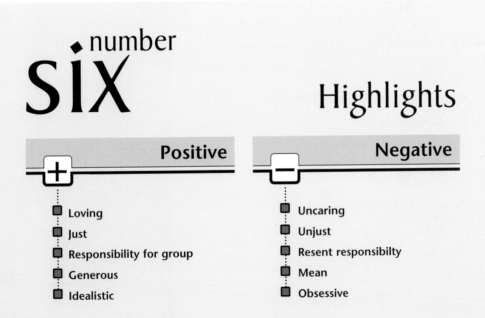

number

six

Highlights

Positive	Negative
+	**—**
Loving	Uncaring
Just	Unjust
Responsibility for group	Resent responsibilty
Generous	Mean
Idealistic	Obsessive

number
seven

Number 7 is the number for rest, trust, fusion, magic and materialization.

□ **Countries**

Sweden, Greece, Bolivia, Peru, Scotland, Philippines, Netherlands.

□ **Famous 7s**

Lauren Bacall, Roger Moore, Marilyn Monroe, Bruce Lee.

Personality

☐ Positive

With a 7 personality you are highly intuitive, and you may even be telepathic. You are a sensitive person.

You are methodical and very organized, and you are also courteous. You are analytical and a perfectionist. You may pay great attention to detail, and you are often fastidious in your appearance.

You are an introspective person who likes to take time to think and ponder on life. You are a private person, and you may be a loner who needs your own space.

You can be dreamy, and you have a vivid imagination. You love nature.

With the 7 you are an instigator, with a practical ability to materialize things and make things happen 'at the drop of a hat'. You project an air of wealth and even when you don't have pots of money in the bank people think you do!

With a 7 you can also be very spiritual and have a keen interest in the 'New Age', its concepts and ideas.

☐ Negative

With a 7 personality, you are prone to self-centredness. You can be too introspective at times, and you often feel isolated, distant, disconnected from people, and cut off from life. You can also be gloomy and negative about your life.

You are a dreamer. You may have a tendency to 'sit on the fence' when opportunities come your way, and watch them drift by.

Alternatively, at times when you are grounded and 'down to earth', you can develop an overriding preoccupation with making money and material possessions.

Under the 7's influence you may be a difficult person, who is picky and notices every little imperfection. You may also have an inferiority complex and never feel 'good enough' at anything.

You often feel hypersensitive and emotionally vulnerable. At times when you are feeling sensitive you can be rude and hurtful to people. You can be naive, and have a childlike view of the world, and can often be 'taken in' by life and people.

Life Path

☐ **Positive**
With a 7 influencing your Life Path you are learning to appreciate what you have, and to appreciate life. You are also learning to trust yourself and to trust others, and to find your own truth in life.

☐ **Negative**
With a 7 Life Path you are impatient and distrusting of people and life. You may evade the truth or be untruthful, and you may take life for granted and show a lack of appreciation towards others.

Wisdom

☐ **Positive**

With a 7 Wisdom Number your practical gift is being able to visualize things very clearly. You are a visionary who has strong intuition and you often receive your guidance through visual dreams.

☐ **Negative**

With a 7 influencing your Wisdom Number you are unable to see clearly, or 'see through' situations or people, and do not follow your intuition or inner vision.

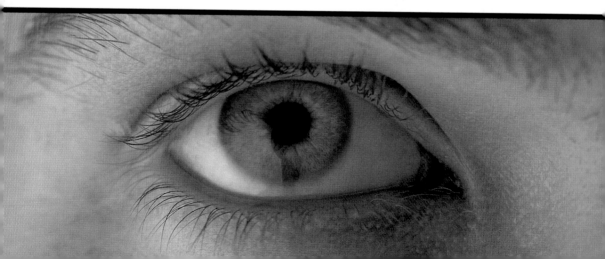

How the number seven influences your:

☐ Health
You are generally robust, but as a result of your sensitive nature your body can get out of balance quickly and you may get sick. You enjoy Tai Chi or gentle yoga, which can help you to keep your delicate energies balanced.

☐ Relationships
You are very choosy, and will wait for the right person to come along before you settle down. You may overanalyze your relationships, and constantly worry about what's not going right instead of appreciating what you have.

☐ Career
You would excel as a recruitment officer, agent, teacher, healer, psychologist, philosopher or a producer. You may also be a city analyst, administrator, researcher, photographer, chemist or surgeon.

□ Finance

When you are grounded and 'down to earth' you can materialize a small fortune with your strong mind and positive thoughts. When you are dreamy you may materialize little, and what you do earn may slip through your fingers.

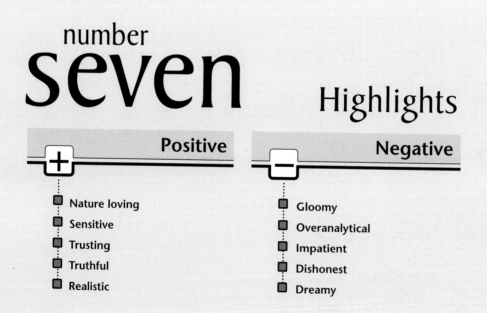

number
seven
Highlights

Positive	Negative
Nature loving	Gloomy
Sensitive	Overanalytical
Trusting	Impatient
Truthful	Dishonest
Realistic	Dreamy

eight
number

Eight is the number for infinity, victory, karma and money.

☐ Countries

Argentina, Poland, China, Alaska, Papua New Guinea, Greenland.

☐ Famous 8s

Marlon Brando, Tatum O'Neil, Barbra Streisand, Shirley Bassey.

Personality

eight
number

☐ **Positive**

With an 8 personality you have enormous amounts of energy, which you direct with your driving ambition towards your goals.

You work extremely hard and with your business flair can make a great success out of whatever goals you attempt. This can, and often does, bring you recognition or even fame.

You are a born organizer. You stride through life with force and direction. At other times you can be passive, when you have exhausted yourself, for example. You can be quite a serious person, and you also take your responsibilities seriously. You like to re-evaluate your life, and to take stock and weigh up other people and situations regularly.

You are practical, realistic and materialistic. You may have an abiding interest in money, fast cars and status, and have a strong sexual identity.

You are a charming and magnetic person. You may be interested in spirituality, which helps you to find inner happiness from the outer achievements in your life.

☐ Negative

You are a stubborn person who at times likes to manipulate others and to get your own way. You are impatient, and you can be very hard on yourself and on others. You can be bossy, aggressive, argumentative, and even a bully at times.

You crave authority. You may be arrogant and flaunt your money, possessions, or your partner in public, to try to boost your self-esteem and make you look good.

You have a great need for recognition. You may be egotistical and conceited, particularly when you do achieve your goals.

You can be an intense and 'heavy' person, and you may be grumpy at times. Sometimes you can be deadly serious about life, and you may take yourself deadly seriously too.

When you don't succeed within certain areas of your life, you can experience great frustration. This lack of success can come about because you refuse to take stock of your life and look at what is happening around you.

Life Path

eight
^{number}

◻ **Positive**

With an 8 Life Path you are learning to develop strength, to be an inspiration both to yourself and others, and to learn to handle power in a positive way.

◻ **Negative**

With the 8 influencing your Life Path you can be weak, and lack inspiration, and you may feel powerless and unable to cope with life.

Wisdom number eight

□ **Positive**

   With the influence of the 8 in
   your Wisdom Number you have a
   practical gift of stamina, and can
   go on and on in pursuit of goals.

□ **Negative**

   Portraying the negative
   influences of the 8 in your
   Wisdom Number may mean
   you lack stamina or drive.

How the **eight** number influences your:

☐ **Health**

You are generally strong and robust. However, you work hard at life, and can push yourself too far so that sometimes you become sick. For relaxation you may watch ballet, gymnastics or motor racing, all of which display control and power, which appeal to you.

☐ **Relationships**

You are highly magnetic, and you tend to attract to you successful, powerful people who have strong identities. Generally you require a partner to be able to 'stand on his or her own two feet' and to be independent.

☐ **Career**

Money is an important issue, so a career as an accountant, or in a financial institution would be ideal. You may also make a good lawyer, librarian, administrator or secretary.

☐ Finance

You like to have pots of money sitting in the bank. With your driving ambition you can amply satisfy your needs, when you are prepared to work for them. Money gives you security and makes you feel powerful.

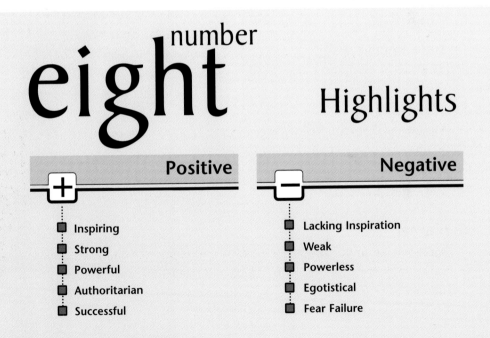

number

eight

Highlights

Positive	Negative
+	**−**
■ Inspiring	■ Lacking Inspiration
■ Strong	■ Weak
■ Powerful	■ Powerless
■ Authoritarian	■ Egotistical
■ Successful	■ Fear Failure

number nine

Nine is the number for endings, new beginnings and transformation.

☐ Countries

Syria, Ireland, Iraq.

☐ Famous 9s

Mahatma Gandhi, Yoko Ono, Paul McCartney, Kevin Costner.

Personality

☐ Positive

With a 9 personality you are a very 'fair' person, and you like to see justice done by everyone. You have a keen sense of judgement, but you do not express these judgements to hurt or infringe on the behaviour of others.

You have your own definite beliefs about life, particularly on religious, political, social and environmental issues. You also have a powerful intellect, which likes to be stimulated by learning about issues that concern the whole world because this helps to educate you.

You are a warm, open and friendly person who is interested in the welfare of others. You have an 'inner knowing', and you use your psychic abilities and your strong instincts.

You have a strong mind that helps to balance out your emotions when you are feeling sensitive. You like to 'fit in' with everybody, and for people to like you. You can be conformist.

With a 9 you are an optimistic person who is adaptable to change. You are practical, with enormous amounts of common sense.

You make a powerful teacher, and people are often inspired to follow the example you set, as a charitable human being.

☐ Negative

With a 9 personality you are judgemental and you constantly criticize yourself and others. You like to feel 'superior' and you can be highly sarcastic and unpleasant in your remarks at times. You can be prone to selfishness.

Sometimes, you can end up preaching at people rather than teaching them, and you may come across as a know-all. You can be impractical at times and lack common sense.

With a 9 you may also find you lack the courage of your convictions, and you may remain non-committal when people ask you to give your point of view.

You may be constantly seeking approval from your partner, friends and family. You may show a lack of understanding towards them when they are in difficult situations, and feel resentment towards helping them at times.

With a 9 you can also be highly secretive and hold onto information that you hear, or knowledge that you gain, and use it for your own ends.

Life Path number nine

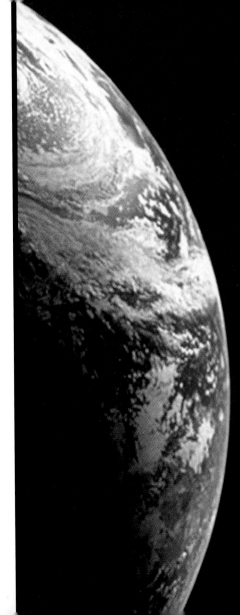

☐ Positive

With a 9 Life Path you are learning to develop selflessness and to care for humanity and the world. Selflessness means 'not thinking of yourself' all the time and looking at the larger picture.

☐ Negative

You may be extremely selfish, with no interest in caring for people, or even possess a careless attitude towards the world in which you live.

Wisdom

number
nine

☐ Positive

With a 9 Wisdom Number your practical gift is the ability to discriminate about facts and life in a positive way. For example, being able to discriminate between whether to cross the road when there is no traffic, or to cross the road when there is traffic, is essential, and can prolong your life if you make the right judgement!

☐ Negative

You may be unable to discriminate about life and situations, as you may be too emotional at times.

How the number **nine** influences your:

☐ Health

You are an open and relaxed person who takes life easy. You generally take good care of yourself. You are very sporty and you may enjoy competing in professional events. Swimming, tennis, rugby, football, polo … you enjoy most things.

☐ Relationships

You are idealistic and generally seek a partner to whom you can make a strong commitment. You are a moralistic person who may believe strongly in family values, and the marriage ritual. You are passionate and a true, loving romantic.

☐ Career

You may be a humanitarian, environmentalist, or doctor. You can excel as a teacher. You may be an artist, musician, a great literary writer or academic, judge or diplomat.

❏ Finance

When you are open to life you tend to attract money to you. You like saving your money for a rainy day. You are as likely to give your money to charity or an environmental cause as you are to give it to your family.

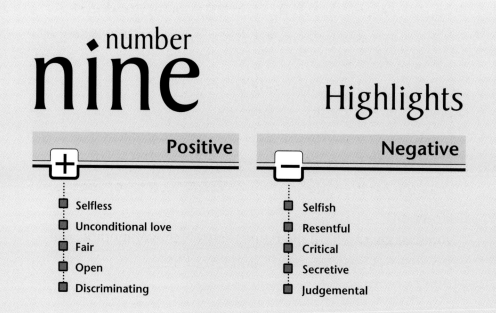

number nine

Highlights

Positive	Negative
+	**−**
Selfless	Selfish
Unconditional love	Resentful
Fair	Critical
Open	Secretive
Discriminating	Judgemental

A Final Word

Now you have read this book you know a little more about numbers, and that they are not simply black and white calculations on a page, but are energies that spring to life with hidden messages, meanings and influences. Potent numbers that can reveal strengths, weaknesses and potential within the cycles they represent.

There are many different ways in which you can experience Numerology. You can have a personal reading from a Numerologist, or you can take part in a group workshop or course. You can even find accurate inspirational material about your chart on the Internet or you can learn from books (right here!)

Numerology can help everyone, and whichever method you use, it can help you grow and enrich your life.

Useful Addresses

AUSTRALIA
Character Analysis and Numerology
Mrs C Anschutz
23 Flinders Street
Kent Town
5067
S. Australia

FRANCE
Christian Gilles School
Residence de L'Abbey Royale
17 Rue Pirel
93200 Saint Denis
PARIS

NEW ZEALAND
Francie Williams
North Shore Parapsychology School
60 East Coast Bay Road
Milford
00649 4101182

UNITED KINGDOM

Association Internationale de Numerologues (A.I.N.)
8 Melbourn Street
Royston
Hertfordshire
SG8 7BZ
www.numerology.org.uk

Connaissance School of Numerology
8 Melbourn Street
Royston
Hertfordshire
SG8 7BZ

UNITED STATES

Marina D Graham
7266 Bennett Valley Road
Santa Rosa
CA 95404-9738